THE 12 Mysteries OF SCRIPTURE

W. E. VINE

The 12 Mysteries of Scripture
By: W. E. Vine, M.A.
Copyright © 2016
GOSPEL FOLIO PRESS
All Rights Reserved

Originally published by: Pickering & Inglis
14 Paternoster Row, London, E.C. 4
229 Bothwell Street, Glasgow, C. 2
29 George IV Bridge, Edinburgh

Published by Gospel Folio Press
304 Killaly St. West Port Colborne, ON L3K 6A6

ISBN: 9781927521656

Cover design by Danielle Robins

All Scripture quotations from the
King James Version unless otherwise noted.

Printed in Canada

Index

Preface

The following pages open up in a very helpful way the "Mysteries of Scripture", and as they one by one are brought before us there rests upon us, surely, no light responsibility, when we consider that God is thus dealing with us as His friends. We recall those words, spoken so long ago, "...*Shall I hide from Abraham that thing which I do*" (Gen. 18:17) and we ask ourselves whether we, like Abraham, are in that attitude of soul before Him which renders possible such communications of His mind and purpose, and bears its issue in like fruit in life and lip. He was a pilgrim, he was able to once without reserve meet His Lord, and he was able to refresh that glorious Visitor. If this is true of us we shall find, as he did, that the "*secret of the Lord is with them that fear him*" (Ps. 25:14), and entering thus into His purpose we shall be more devoted to His interests, and be able, like Abraham, to intercede for the lost and perishing around us. "*Henceforth I call you not servants; for the servant knoweth not what his lord doeth: but I have called you friends; for all things that I have heard of my Father I have made known unto you*" (John 15:15). If it is as stewards that we have been put in trust with the mysteries of God, "*it is required in stewards, that a man be found faithful*" (1 Cor. 4:2). May it be so for His Name's sake.   —W. R. Lewis, Bath

Introduction

The word "mystery" in Scripture does not denote that which is mysterious. Its meaning therefore differs from that of its current use in English. In Scripture it denotes that which, being outside the range of unassisted natural apprehension, can be made known only by divine revelation, and is made known in a manner and at a time appointed by God, and to those only who are illumined by His Spirit. In the ordinary sense a mystery implies knowledge withheld; its Scriptural significance is truth revealed. Hence the terms especially associated with the subject are "made known", "manifested", "revealed", "preached", "understand", "dispensation". The definition given above may be best illustrated by the following passages: *"Even the mystery which hath been hid from ages and from generations, but now is made manifest to his saints"* (Col. 1:26); *"...the mystery of Christ...Which in other ages was not made known unto the sons of men, as it is now revealed unto his holy apostles and prophets by the Spirit"* (Eph. 3:4-5); *"...the mystery, which was kept secret since the world began, But now is made manifest, and by the scriptures of the prophets, according to the commandment of the everlasting God, made known to all nations for the obedience of faith"* (Rom. 16:25-26).

PAGAN MYSTERIES

In the heathen religion of the Greeks, mysteries consisted of a set of rites and ceremonies esteemed as peculiarly sacred, and observed with the strictest secrecy. Membership of the societies which practised them was open to any who desired to be initiated, granted the fulfilment of the necessary conditions. Those who had passed through the various stages of initiation were known as "the perfected". This was probably present to the mind of Paul when he said, *"Howbeit we speak wisdom among **them that are perfect**: yet not the wisdom of this world, nor of the princes of this world, that come to nought: But we speak the wisdom of God in a mystery, even the hidden wisdom, which God ordained before the world unto our glory...we* *have received, not the spirit of the world, but the spirit which is of God; that we might know the things that are freely given to us of God"* (1 Cor. 2:6-7, 12). This all stands in striking contrast to the methods of secrecy adopted by the priests of the heathen mysteries. Contrast also the following: *"But have renounced the hidden things of dishonesty, not walking in craftiness, nor handling the word of God deceitfully; but by manifestation of the truth commending ourselves to every man's conscience in the sight of God"* (2 Cor. 4:2).

(a)
Mysteries Relating to the Word of God

*"Likewise must the deacons be grave, not double-tongued, not given to much wine, not greedy of filthy lucre; Holding **the mystery of the faith** in a pure conscience."*   1 Timothy 3:8-9

"Beloved, when I gave all diligence to write unto you of the common salvation, it was needful for me to write unto you, and exhort you that ye should earnestly contend for the faith which was once delivered unto the saints."   Jude 3

CHAPTER ONE
The Mystery of the Faith

1 Timothy 3:8-9, Jude 3

Among the qualifications essential for those who render service as deacons is that of holding *"the mystery of the faith"* in a good conscience (1 Tim. 3:9). The faith is the sum, or body, of Christian doctrine, *"...once delivered unto the saints"* (Jude 3). This mystery therefore embraces all the other, and suitably comes first for our consideration. Revealed in the Person and work of Christ and by the Spirit of God to His apostles, and recorded in the New Testament, the faith had been kept secret be God in preceding ages, until the advent of the One in whom its doctrines were to centre. There was "a fullness of the time" for the revelation of the faith; the doctrines pertaining to it had been embodied and somewhat dimly foreshadowed in the Old Testament; the clear enunciation was commenced by Christ Himself in the days of His flesh, and completed by His apostles.

WHY "THE MYSTERY OF THE FAITH"?

The faith is so called because it is given as the object of faith. That which God reveals demands acceptance and necessitates faith. But faith is a spiritual activity, and spiritual apprehension is required for spiritual truths. *" But the natural man receiveth not the things of the Spirit of God: for they are foolishness unto him: neither can he know them, because they are spiritually discerned"* (1 Cor. 2:14). The reception of the faith is essentially the work of the Spirit of God, and He it is who prepares the heart to receive it, in the acceptance of Christ by faith, on the ground of the necessity and sufficiency of His vicarious sacrifices as the means of the remission of sins.

Now all this fulfils the conditions which characterize a Scripture mystery. There was (1) a period of divine reticence, the faith not being then made fully known; (2) an appointed time for revelation, through the coming of Christ, and His preparation and commission of His apostles to announce the faith; (3) a communication made to special recipients of the mystery (in this case to all who through the operation of the Spirit accept the gospel).

(b)
Mysteries Relating to the Son of God

"*For I would that ye knew what great conflict I have for you, and for them at Laodicea, and for as many as have not seen my face in the flesh; That their hearts might be comforted, being knit together in love, and unto all riches of the full assurance of understanding, to the acknowledgement of* **the mystery of God, and of the Father, and of Christ;** *In whom are hid all the treasures of wisdom and knowledge... Beware lest any man spoil you through philosophy and vain deceit, after the tradition of men, after the rudiments of the world, and not after Christ. For in him dwelleth all the fulness of the Godhead bodily. And ye are complete in him, which is the head of all principality and power...*" Colossians 2:1-3, 8-10

CHAPTER TWO

The Godhead of Christ

Colossians 2:1-3, 8-10

Two mysteries involve doctrines concerning the Son of God. The first is called "the mystery of God", the second "the mystery of godliness". The first is described as follows: *"the mystery of God, and of the Father, and of Christ"* (Col. 2:2). That is to say, the mystery of God is the Father and the Christ, expressing the Duo-unity of the Father and the Son (just as there is a Tri-unity, or Trinity, of the Godhead in the Father, the Son, and the Spirit). This divine unity is beyond human conception save by special revelation of God. Christ came to give the revelation. Early in His ministry He declared that *"... no man knoweth the Son, but the Father; neither knoweth any man the Father, save the Son, and he to whomsoever the Son will reveal him"* (Matt. 11:27). To His unity with the Father He bore testimony to the unbelieving Pharisees: *"I and my Father are one"* (John 10:30); and again to the disciples, who heard it perhaps most impressively when, in prayer to the Father, He said, *"that they may be one, as we are"* (John 17:11); and again, *"And the glory which thou gavest me I have given them; that they may be one, even as we are one"* (John 17:22).

CHRIST IN JOHN'S GOSPEL

In the introduction of John's gospel (in which it was especially allotted to that writer to present the Saviour as the Son of God) Christ is thus strikingly brought before us as the Revealer of this mystery: *"No man hath seen God at any time; the only begotten Son, which is in the bosom of the Father, he hath declared him"* (John 1:18).

In the text of the Revised Version, in Colossians 2:2, the mystery of God is defined as *"Christ"*, and this is supported first, by the context, and, second, by the general teaching of the epistle. For, first, the apostle immediately says that *"In whom are hid all the treasures of wisdom and knowledge"* (Col. 2:3). Christ is the Depository in and through whom have been, and will be, revealed all that God wills to reveal. And, second, the aim of the epistle is to present the Deity, majesty, prerogatives, and power of the Son of God, and so to show that through His redemptive sacrifice, and in Him as our risen Head, we are completely supplied with all we need. Accordingly, in a sentence which forms the key to the whole epistle, we are told that *"...in him dwelleth all the fulness of the Godhead bodily. And ye are complete in him"* (Col. 2:9-10). The fulness of the Godhead is not something that was bestowed upon the Son. Nor did Christ ever "assume Deity". Its fullness ever abode in Him, and remained in Him when, partaking of flesh and blood, He became Man, perfect humanity and absolute Deity being combined. That is what is implied in the emphasis the apostle lays upon the word *"bodily"*. The word *"fulness"* does not here mean a filling up. It signifies unoriginated totality.

ASSURANCE OF THE MYSTERY

This, then, is the mystery into which we are to enter, with *"...all riches of the full assurance of understanding"* (Col. 2:2), not with a blind acceptance of the doctrine, but in that appreciation of the glory and power of the Son of God which will guard us against being deluded into any of the many errors concerning Him, and so from ceasing to *"holding the Head"* (Col. 2:19).

*"These things write I unto thee, hoping to come unto thee shortly: But if I tarry long, that thou mayest know how thou oughtest to behave thyself in the house of God, which is the church of the living God, the pillar and ground of the truth. And without controversy great is **the mystery of godliness**: God was manifest in the flesh, justified in the Spirit, seen of angels, preached unto the Gentiles, believed on in the world, received up into glory."*

1 Timothy 3:14-16

*"And **the Word was made flesh**, and dwelt among us, (and we beheld his glory, the glory as of the only begotten of the Father,) full of grace and truth."*

John 1:14

*"**And declared to be the Son of God with power, according to the spirit of holiness,** by the resurrection from the dead."*   Romans 1:4

CHAPTER THREE
The Mystery of Godliness
1 Timothy 3:14-16, John 1:14, Romans 1:4

We are now to consider the second mystery relating to the Person of the Son of God. This is called *"the mystery of godliness"* (1 Tim. 3:16), and Paul describes it as "incontrovertibly great". Possibly the words which immediately precede also form part of the description, which then would read thus: *"... the pillar and ground of the truth. And without controversy great is the mystery of godliness"* (1 Tim. 3:15-16). Then follows the definition: *"...He was manifested in the flesh, vindicated by the Spirit, seen by angels, proclaimed among the nations, believed on in the world, taken up in glory"* (1 Tim. 3:16, ESV).

WHY SO TERMED?

The reason why this related to the Person is termed *"the mystery of godliness"* (1 Tim. 3:16) may be ascertained by observing the connection of the passage with the preceding context, and the contrast with the succeeding context, in the latter of which warning is given concerning the coming ungodliness of departure from the faith, through seducing spirits and doctrines of demons. In the preceding context the apostle's subject is the testimony which the church is called to give to the world. The whole passage bears upon that. He has just pointed out the necessity that overseers and deacons should have a good testimony from them that are without, and now is giving instructions as to how men ought to behave in the house of God, which is the church of the living God; that is to say, what should be the conduct of believers, as those who constitute the house of God, in bearing witness to the world, whether by lip or life. A church or assembly is the witness of God to men. Now the essential elements of this witness are the truths concerning Christ, and especially those bearing upon the relations between God and man. The doctrines are not stated merely as so many concrete facts concerning Him; they form the basis of testimony as to godliness, expressed in what is predicated of Christ. For such a witness godliness on the part of those who bear it is essential. Thus the truths which the apostle states concerning Christ form the climax to the exhortations he has been giving concerning godliness. For how can truths which set forth the ground of the relations of God to man be rightly proclaimed by the church of the living God, unless those who constitute it live themselves *"in all godliness"*? (1 Tim. 2:2).

ANOTHER SUGGESTION

It has been suggested that, adopting the marginal reading of the Revised Version *"which was manifested"*, the statements of verse 16, though definitely said of Christ, are, at the same time, in a secondary sense, applicable also to the church, concerning which Paul has just been speaking, and that clauses *"preached unto the Gentiles"* and *"believed on in the world"* (1 Tim. 3:16) may contain a veiled reference to the truth concerning the church and to its testimony respectively. But all this seems like pressing the meaning of the passage beyond its justifiable limits. We must not get away from the immediate application of these great foundation truths regarding the Son of God.

TESTIMONY CONCERNING THE LORD

HIS FLESH

1. He was *"manifest in the flesh"* (1 Tim. 3:16). The introductory word declares His Deity whether directly, as in the Authorized Version, or indirectly in the relative *"who"*, which may be connected with the antecedent *"God"* in verse 15, the intervening words being parenthetic. The word *"He"* does not form part of the original. His pre-existence also is clearly implied. That which is manifested has merely been hidden prior to its manifestation. He was *"...with the Father, and was manifested unto us"* (1 John 1:2). *"And the Word was made flesh, and dwelt among us"* (John 1:14). Identifying Himself with

humanity, apart from sin, He partook of flesh and blood. This was the first step towards the mediatorial relationship between God and man, established by one Mediator, "Himself Man, Christ Jesus". That relationship could only be brought about by His death and resurrection.

HIS SPIRIT

2. He was *"justified in the Spirit"* (1 Tim. 3:16). The Mediator, in order to atone for sin by vicarious sacrifice, must be Himself sinless. The fact of the absence of all sin during the whole of His life has been proved in every possible way, His enemies themselves being witness. His was the spirit of holiness, of absolute freedom from all taint or possibility of defilement. *"...he was manifested to take away our sins; and in him is no sin"* (1 John 3:5). He passed through the fire of fierce temptation unscathed. But how was He justified? Not as we are. We are justified by grace as sinners. He was justified in vindication of His sinlessness. Righteousness is imputed to us; righteousness was inherent in Him. To this the Father bore witness at His baptism and at His transfiguration, and completely vindicated His sinlessness by raising Him from the dead. Thus it was that God justified His Son, and thus was fulfilled the Messianic prophecy of Isaiah: *"He is near that justifieth me"* (Isa. 50:8). He was *"declared to be* (or 'marked out' as) *the Son of God with power, according to the spirit of holiness"* (Rom. 1:4). That declaration was only consistent with His essential and manifested holiness. Albeit every test was applied, He was proved to be the Just One, the Holy One.

THE ANGELS

3. He was *"seen of angels"* (1 Tim. 3:16). Angelic witness is thus added to the divine. This may refer to the angels who witnessed His resurrection. But we are perhaps not safe in limiting the time to that occasion. They had seen Him, had been with Him, and had attended upon Him during the days of His flesh. The mystery of godliness was made evident to

them both during the days of His sorrows and temptations, and in the time of His resurrection glory.

THE NATIONS

4. He was *"preached unto the Gentiles"* (1 Tim. 3:16). The great foundation of the spiritual relationship between God and man having been laid in the incarnation, death, and resurrection of the Son of God, the testimony could now go forth to all the nations. Barriers between Jew and Gentile were broken down. The preaching was not to be merely that of the doctrines of a creed, nor that of godliness in the abstract; it must be that of a Person, godliness incarnate in the Son, incarnate with the one grand object of the redemption of sinners through atonement, and vindicated in His triumphant resurrection. *"...Christ be preached that he rose from the dead"* (1 Cor. 15:12).

THE WORLD

5. He was *"believed on in the world"* (1 Tim. 3:16). The preaching must be the presentation of Christ as the object of faith. Truly He was worthy so to be presented. Man is responsible to accept Him. Faith is the one great essential for men, and the faith of all sorts and conditions of men has reposed in Him. *"Our testimony among you was believed"* (2 Thess. 1:10), wrote Paul to the church of the Thessalonians. The saving faith of the vast multitudes of the redeemed during these nineteen centuries has been one long series of confirmations of the truths of the mystery of godliness centring in and embodied in the Son of God.

THE GLORY

6. He was *"received up into glory"* (1 Tim. 3:16). Thus the Spirit of God through the apostle completes the cycle of this mystery. Christ returned from whence He had come. *"He that descended is the same also that ascended"* (Eph. 4:10). God highly exalted Him to His rightful place, the right hand of the throne of God, *"...the throne of the Majesty in the heavens"* (Heb. 8:1). To sum up, godliness has been manifested, vindicated,

and enthroned, in Him. *"For in him dwelleth all the fulness of the Godhead bodily"* (Col. 2:9), the ever-living and unchanging Christ; it has been manifested in His incarnation, vindicated in His resurrection, and enthroned in His ascension and His intercession at the right hand of the Father.

(c)
Mysteries Relating to the Church of God

*"And take the helmet of salvation, and the sword of the Spirit, which is the word of God: Praying always with all prayer and supplication in the Spirit, and watching thereunto with all perseverance and supplication for all saints; And for me, that utterance may be given unto me, that I may open my mouth boldly, to make known **the mystery of the gospel**, For which I am an ambassador in bonds: that therein I may speak boldly, as I ought to speak."*

Ephesians 6:17-20

*"If ye have heard of the dispensation of the grace of God which is given me to you-ward: How that by revelation he made known unto me **the mystery**; (as I wrote afore in few words, Whereby, when ye read, ye may understand my knowledge in **the mystery of Christ**)."*

Ephesians 3:2-4

CHAPTER FOUR
The Mystery of the Gospel

Ephesians 6:17-20, Ephesians 3:2-4

In writing to the saints at Ephesus Paul requested them to pray for him that utterance might be given him in making known the mystery of the gospel, that he might speak boldly concerning it (Eph. 6:18, 20). It was one of the chief subjects about which he had written to them. The gospel itself is not the mystery; the mystery of the gospel is that which belongs to the gospel, or is comprehended in it. The apostle had called it *"the mystery of Christ"* (Eph. 3:4), and pointed out that a special dispensation (i.e. stewardship) of the grace of God had been given him in regard to it. Its subject may be divided into two parts as follows.

(1) GENTILES BROUGHT INTO THE BODY

THE BODY

Human faculties could never have conceived either the foundation truths of the gospel or the mystery relating to it. Receiving it by divine revelation, Paul had been granted an understanding in it, and the leading feature of it was *"that the Gentiles should be fellowheirs, and of the same body, and partakers of his promise in Christ by the gospel"* (Eph. 3:6). This, he says, had been hidden from the sons of men until God's time came for revealing it to His apostles and prophets (cp. Rom. 16:25-26). Of the special revelation and trust given to Paul himself in the matter, he says: *"Unto me, who am less than the least of all saints, is this grace given, that I should preach among the Gentiles the unsearchable riches of Christ; And to make all men see* (or perhaps as in the margin, 'to bring to light') *what is the fellowship of the mystery, which from the beginning of the world hath been hid in God"* (Eph. 3:8-9).

The wisdom of God is seen in the particular time appointed for the declaration of this mystery. To bring Gentiles into spiritual union with Jews prior to the dispensation of Grace would have nullified the very purposes for which the dispensation of Law was ordained. The middle wall of partition had been built up by God, and separation had to be maintained. Albeit, even while the wall was in existence, blessing for the Gentiles was foretold from time to time, a matter to which Paul directs attention in Romans 10:18-20. The mystery relating to the breaking down of the barrier, and the incorporation of believing Jews and Gentiles into the one body of Christ, was, however, withheld until the divine purposes of the Law had been fulfilled, and the message of full and free salvation through faith in Christ could be sent to all men irrespective of nationality.

SPIRITUAL UNION

We should observe that the leading feature of the mystery is not merely that regenerate Jew and Gentile are brought into joint blessing, but that in Christ, in whom they are no longer Jew and Gentile, they are united in a living, spiritual organism, as His body. Again, the mystery is not the church itself, but its relationship with Christ.

When the apostle uses the illustration of the natural relationship between husband and wife, he says: *"This is a great mystery: but I speak concerning Christ and the church"* (Eph. 5:32). That is to say, the mystery has to do not with the natural relationship, but the spiritual union which it illustrates. All is headed up in Christ. *"Christ is the head of the church: and he is the saviour of the body"* (Eph. 5:23). The church is His fullness; she is His glory. But this is the fullness of One who Himself fills. In and through her are, and are to be displayed, His infinite love, His redeeming grace, and glorious power. In that the church is His fullness, He will present her to Himself; He will rejoice in her spotless beauty as the fruit of His sufferings and the reflection of His own image. In that He fills the church, His splendour will irradiate creation through her; in the day of His manifestation He will come forth to be marvelled at in her. The mystery of the union will be unfolded to wondering worlds.

ETERNAL UNION

But there is a present unfolding, and that to the principalities and powers in the heavenly places. To them *"might be known by the church the manifold wisdom of God"* (or, more literally and expressively, "the much-varied wisdom of God", Eph. 3:10). With admiring interest these angelic beings had watched the dealings of God with man, as the divine plan developed in the ages prior to the period of gospel grace. By variety of action but unity of design, by difference in method but harmony in development, the wisdom of God had been displayed. All, however, was but a preparation for a more stupendous manifestation. The condescension and humiliation of their own Creator, His atoning sufferings for a rebellious man, His triumphant resurrection and ascension, followed by the sending of the Holy Spirit, issued now in a creation far transcending all else that the mind of God ever devised, namely, the formation of a body composed of redeemed sinners, Jew and Gentile, brought from the depths of sin and alienation, and joined to their Redeemer in spiritual and eternal union. Here was the grand culmination of the varied actings of omniscient and manifold wisdom. Now at length was revealed to these heavenly principalities and powers the infinite fullness of love, grace, and power by which that wisdom had operated and was yet to operate. These things the angels desire to look into.

(2) CHRIST IN HIS SAINTS

THE SAINTS

The apostle refers to the same mystery in another way in the Epistle to the Colossians. There he speaks of it as *"Christ in you, the hope of glory"* (Col. 1:27). In Ephesians the prominent thought is the union of the saints in Christ: in Colossians it is the indwelling of Christ in the saints; in Ephesians the union of Jew and Gentile in one body is chiefly in view; in Colossians attention is more particularly called to a special feature of the mystery, namely, that in Gentiles, formerly *"alienated and enemies"* (Col. 1:21), Christ now invisibly dwells. In both Epistles the figure is that of the body of which Christ is the Head (Col. 1:18). Here again Paul speaks of the stewardship committed to him. For the sake of the body, the church, he had been made a minister according to the stewardship given him *"to fulfil the word of God"* (Col. 1:25), even the mystery, formerly hid, but now manifested to His saints, *"To whom God would make known what is the riches of the glory of this mystery among the Gentiles; which is Christ in you, the hope of glory"* (Col. 1:27).

THE CYCLES OF DOCTRINES

We should not fail to observe that in unfolding this mystery the apostle describes himself as fulfilling the Word of God. This cannot mean the fulfillment of his service in the gospel; for to declare the mystery was something more than to preach the gospel. Nor can it mean the fulfilment of the promise of God; for the truth of the mystery exceeded the promises, inasmuch as it had never been made known before. The declaration of this transcendent truth was the completion of the whole cycle of the doctrines given in the Word of God. The Scriptures written later, by the apostle John, for example, either revealed in a new light what had already been communicated, or supplemented the doctrines of this mystery. The mystery. The mystery of the union of Gentile with Jew in the body of Christ has to do with the interval between Pentecost and the Lord's Second Coming; and the special revelation entrusted to Paul not only set forth the divine counsels concerning that interval, but gave finality to all the revelations of the Word of God.

"And when he was alone, they that were about him with the twelve asked of him the parable. And he said unto them, Unto you it is given to know **the mystery of the kingdom of God**: but unto them that are without, all these things are done in parables."

Mark 4:10-11

"...Because it is given unto you to know **the mysteries of the kingdom of heaven**, but to them it is not given." Matthew 13:11

CHAPTER FIVE

The Mystery of the Kingdom
Mark 4:10-11, Matthew 13:11

This forms the subject of the parables recorded in Matthew 13, Mark 4, and Luke 8. In Matthew the Lord speaks of the mysteries of the kingdom of heaven (lit., "of the heavens"); in Luke, *"the kingdom of God"* (Luke 17:20-21); in Mark they are summed up as *"the mystery of the kingdom of God"* (Mark 4:11). The terms *"the kingdom of God"* and "the kingdom of the heavens" are frequently interchangeable (cp. Matt. 19:23 with v. 24; Matt. 10:14 with Mark 10:14; Matt. 13:11 with Luke 8:10), but are not entirely identical in significance. Now is the difference merely titular, though they do differ in this respect, the one speaking of the King Himself, the other of the sphere of His sovereignty. A glance at the references mentioned above shows the inaccuracy of the supposed differentiation that while the kingdom of heaven includes evil principles with good, the kingdom of God contains the good alone.

"THE KINGDOM OF GOD"

"The kingdom of God" (Luke 17:20-21) is a general term for the kingdom in all its aspects, in all dispensations, and viewed whether in the past eternity, or during the periods of human rebellion prior to, and including, the rejection of Christ as the King, or in the present age in which the kingdom is in mystery, or in the coming age when it will be in manifestation, or in the ages beyond. "The kingdom of heaven" is a comparative term, implying the existence of a contrary sphere and contrary principles of operation. In this respect it is of course identical with the kingdom of God in one of its phases, since the latter is descriptive of the kingdom of all times. The phrase *"the kingdom of heaven"* is confined to Matthew's gospel, where it occurs some twenty-five times. Its

use there shows a constant reference, expressed or implied, to antagonistic forces. The opposing element is prominent in the parables of Matthew 13, which treat that period in which the kingdom is in a mystery. That it should be in mystery was immediately due to the rejection of the King by the Jews. For this they were temporarily cast away (Rom. 11:15), and the offer of submission to the King and entrance into His kingdom was made to men of every nationality. The kingdom has not, and does not, yet come with outward manifestation (Luke 17:20, margin).

THE CHURCH AND CHRISTENDOM

The church is not coextensive with the kingdom of heaven. The church has its part therein, but when it is removed the operations of the kingdom will continue in the earth. At the present time Christendom may be said to be coextensive with the kingdom in its mystery phase; that phase comprises all who, whether in reality or profession, make some acknowledgment of Christ. All this is evidenced in the scope of the parables setting forth the mysteries of the kingdom. In the first parable, that of the sower, the general principles of the kingdom are symbolized in their activities in the world during the rejection of the King. In the next three, those of the tares, the mustard seed, and the leaven, the outward aspect of the kingdom is presented. In each the forces of evil are seen at work.

THE PARABLE OF THE TARES

The Lord's explanation of this parable draws our attention to final issues. The tares are bound in bundles by the servants (perhaps indicating ungodly associations), and left in the field for the time prior to their being burned; the wheat is taken into the garner. The true are removed before judgment is executed on the false, the binding in bundles being a preparatory step to that. The saints are to possess the kingdom, but that does not take place until *"all things that offend, and them which do iniquity"* (Matt. 13:41) have been cast out of it. In the parables of the sower and the tares the individual is especially in view; the parables of the leaven and the mustard seed have a collective aspect. The last three parables were spoken privately to the disciples. The first two of these, relating to the treasure and the pearl, present the inward aspect of the kingdom, and bring into greater prominence the divine appreciation of that which is true and genuine therein. In the last parable, relating to the net, the principles of the kingdom and their operations are again viewed in their ultimate issues, evil being purged out of it.

THE KINGDOM OF HEAVEN

Thus the Lord unfolds the secret of the kingdom of heaven during the period in which it exists in mystery. Throughout this period the forces of darkness work within the sphere of the operations of the kingdom, the former operating from beneath the latter from above. Hence the significances of the expression "the kingdom of the heavens". The earth is the immediate arena of the conflict, and there Satan aims at absolute dominion. But "the heavens bear rule". The Adversary will not ultimately triumph. The darkness will not overpower the light. The King will intervene in Person. Satan will be bound and consigned to the abyss, and his human instruments will be destroyed. The mystery phase will be over, and the kingdom of God will be in manifested glory. *"Then shall the righteous shine forth as the sun in the kingdom of their Father"* (Matt. 13:43).

"And I turned to see the voice that spake with me. And being turned, I saw seven golden candlesticks; And in the midst of the seven candlesticks one like unto the Son of man, clothed with a garment down to the foot, and girt about the paps with a golden girdle. His head and his hairs were white like wool, as white as snow; and his eyes were as a flame of fire; And his feet like unto fine brass, as if they burned in a furnace; and his voice as the sound of many waters. And he had in his right hand seven stars: and out of his mouth went a sharp twoedged sword: and his countenance was as the sun shineth in his strength. And when I saw him, I fell at his feet as dead."   Revelation 1:12-17

CHAPTER SIX

The Mystery of the Seven Stars and Lampstands

Revelation 1:12-17

The mystery of the seven stars and lampstands of the opening vision in the Book of Revelation, in which Christ was seen walking in the midst of the lampstands, was interpreted by the Lord Himself. Other beings were employed by Him in the interpretation of later visions; these were of a different character from that of the first, which was connected directly with the church. An angel, for instance, explained the symbolism of the woman and the beast in chapter 17. That the Lord in Person revealed the meaning of the symbols relating to the churches seems to be indicative of their intimate relationship with Himself and of His jealous care for them.

THE SEVEN CHURCHES OF ASIA

His description of the seven stars and the seven golden lampstands as a mystery suggests that the seven churches in Asia and their angels, or messengers, had a significance beyond their immediate individuality and locality. This is confirmed in several ways.

LETTERS FOR ALL

1. The very title of the books shows it. It is *"The Revelation of Jesus Christ, which God gave unto him, to shew unto his servants things which must shortly come to pass"* (Rev. 1:1). Thus the contents of the seven letters to the churches were for all the Lord's people.

TO HEAR AND HEED

2. In each of the seven He calls upon all who are His to give heed to the messages: *"He that hath an ear, let him hear what the Spirit saith unto the churches"* (Rev. 2:29).

—FOR ALL TIME

3. Whatever view may be taken of the application of these seven letters, whether, for instance, they represent successive periods of church history, or whether simultaneous spiritual conditions are set forth, the very character of the letters indicates a more comprehensive scope than that of the localities mentioned.

PROGRESSIVE PHASES

4. The churches appear to have been selected, and the various messages framed, with respect to the conditions prevailing in each assembly, in order to convey truth applicable to churches generally throughout the present era, and to set forth the responsibilities attaching to testimony—all as beneath the searching gaze and in the unerring estimating of the Lord. There are evidences, indeed, that progressive phases of church testimony generally throughout the dispensation are in view, but consideration of those lies beyond the limits of this chapter.

COMPLETE COUNSEL

5. The number seven in the Scripture clearly suggests totality, universality, and completeness. Thus the numerical significance here indicates that the seven churches were representative of local churches everywhere and at all times, and of prevailing characteristics of the church at any particular period.

THE ANGELS OF THE CHURCHES

The angels of the churches were those to whom the seven letters were immediately addressed. That these angels were seen as stars perhaps suggests that they are heavenly beings, as distinct from the earthly symbolism of the lampstands. Something may also be said for the view that the seven stars symbolize ideal spirits characterizing the churches. It must be remembered, however, that the Greek word, often simply means a "messenger". Possibly, therefore, we are not to press the heavenly aspect of the symbol, but to regard the messengers as the human instruments in conveying orally the messages. The persons to whom would be entrusted the reading of the letter would be under an extremely solemn responsibility, for these messages came from the risen and ascended Lord Himself, and through an apostle whose words were divinely inspired. In this, it may be, lies the significance of the declaration at the beginning of the Book: *"Blessed is he that readeth"* (Rev. 1:3), i.e., publicly. The reader as the deliverer of the message would be the messenger to the church. If that is so, the stars may be regarded as symbolizing the means of giving the light of the revealed thoughts and counsels of the Lord to the saints in the churches.

THE LAMPSTANDS

The symbolism of the lampstands is to be distinguished from what is set forth by similar imagery in the Old Testament, inasmuch as a mystery involves the revelation of something not previously made known. Each lampstand is set upon its own base, in contradistinction to the one lampstand in the Tabernacle. Each church is responsible, independently of the others, to the Lord, who judges each separately. At the same time He has a common relationship to all, a relationship of authority involving the approbation or disapprobation of what is pleasing or displeasing to Him, and a recompense according to works. He walks amidst the lampstands. They, again, are lights not in the sanctuary but in the world. The responsibility of testimony is in view, and the testimony is regarded externally and historically. It therefore seems to include profession as well as reality. Sardis, for instance, had a name to live, but was dead. Laodicea so failed that the Lord took His stand outside. Thus, as with the parables in Matthew 13, this mystery, though distinct from the mysteries of the kingdom, is seen to contain the admixture of evil with good, of corruption with purity, of error with truth, of loyal devotion to Christ with declension from His will, such as has been and is evidenced in what is known as Christendom.

(d)
Mysteries Relating to Apostasy from God

"Behold, I shew you a mystery; We shall not all sleep, but we shall all be changed, In a moment, in the twinkling of an eye, at the last trump: for the trumpet shall sound, and the dead shall be raised incorruptible, and we shall be changed. For this corruptible must put on incorruption, and this mortal must put on immortality. So when this corruptible shall have put on incorruption, and this mortal shall have put on immortality, then shall be brought to pass the saying that is written, Death is swallowed up in victory. O death, where is thy sting? O grave, where is thy victory? The sting of death is sin; and the strength of sin is the law. But thanks be to God, which giveth us the victory through our Lord Jesus Christ."   1 Corinthians 15:51-57

CHAPTER SEVEN

The Transformation of the Bodies of the Saints at the Resurrection

1 Corinthians 15:51-57

We are now to consider the last of the group of mysteries connected with the church. The first, the mystery of the gospel, relates to its formation, the last relates to its consummation. *"Behold,"* says the apostle, *"I shew you a mystery; We shall not all sleep, but we shall all be changed, In a moment, in the twinkling of an eye, at the last trump: for the trumpet shall sound, and the dead shall be raised incorruptible, and we shall be changed. For this corruptible must put on incorruption, and this mortal must put on immortality"* (1 Cor. 15:51-53).

THE RESURRECTION IS NOT A MYSTERY

It should be observed that the resurrection itself is not a "mystery". Many revelations predicting that event had been given prior to the special instruction imparted to Paul. Job knew that his body would be raised from the dead (Ps. 16:9-11; 17:15). The resurrection of saints collectively was prophesied by Isa. 25:8), and by Hosea (13:14), and was made known to Daniel (12:2). The Lord predicted it in fuller detail, both publicly to the Jews (John 5:28-29; 6:39, 44), and privately to His disciples (John 11:24-26; 14:19). Martha's words to the Lord concerning Lazarus, *"I know that he shall rise again in the resurrection at the last day"* (John 11:24), and the ironical reference by the Sadducees to *"the resurrection"* (Matt. 22:30) show that the doctrine of the resurrection was commonly accepted, save by those who formed or followed the sect of the Sadducees. The doctrine was regularly taught by the Pharisees (Acts 23:6, 8). It constituted an essential truth of the gospel preached by the apostles (Acts 4:2). And in this chapter of 1 Corinthians it is the subject of Paul's main argument up to this point.

He has something now to add beyond the fact that there will be a resurrection of the saints, something not hitherto made known, namely, that not all the saints will fall asleep, but that the bodies of all, whether of those who have fallen asleep, or those who are alive, will together be changed.[1]

A NEW REVELATION

This change involves resurrection for those whose bodies have died, but the point of the mystery is the simultaneous transformation of the bodies of all. That this was a new revelation is confirmed by the passage in 1 Thessalonians 4, where the apostle, predicting the same event, declares that it was made known to him by the word of the Lord (lit., by a word of the Lord), that is to say, not by the Scriptures, but by a revelation from the ascended Christ.

This particular truth, like the mystery of the body of Christ, seems to have been committed to Paul to be made known to the church. There is no indication of its having been revealed before. In the Thessalonian passage we are taught that one event will follow another; first the resurrection of those who have fallen asleep, then the simultaneous rapture of all. In 1 Corinthians 15:51-53 the leading idea is the instantaneous transformation of all—the corruptible, the body upon which death has passed, putting on incorruption, and the mortal, the body liable to death, but without the actual experience of it, putting on immortality, and all taking place *"In a moment, in the twinkling of an eye"* (1 Cor. 15:52).

THE LAST TRUMP

This mystery is to have fulfilment *"at the last trump"* (1 Cor. 15:52), the only indication here given of the time of the

---

1   It would always be better to translate by "fall asleep", "fallen asleep", etc., than simply by "sleep", save, of course, in Daniel 12:2, where reference is to the body. See the Revised Version of Matthew 27:52, John 11:11, and 1 Thess. 4:13-15. To be consistent the revisers should have similarly rendered the verb by *"fall asleep"* in 1 Corinthians 15:51.

occurrence. The assumption that this trump is identical with the last in the series of trumpets mentioned in Revelation, chapters 8, 9, and 11, is gratuitous. The trumpets of the Apocalypse, like the seals and vials, are symbolic. Paul is not speaking in the symbolism of visions. His language, if figurative, is metaphorical rather than symbolic. But this passage, compared with 1 Thessalonians 4:16, suggests the actual sounding of a trumpet. Moreover, the visions in the Apocalypse were of later date than 1 Corinthians.

"The last trump" may be a military metaphor, and possibly has reference to the trumpets mentioned in Numbers 10:2-6, by which the people of Israel were either assembled or received notice that the camp was to move forward. On the other hand, the *"last trump"* may stand in contrast with the trump of Sinai. The subject of the Law was so constant in the apostle's teaching and writings that an indirect reference to the occasion would be readily grasped by the readers without further explanation.

THE TWO TRUMPETS

Further, that the two trumpets should be distinguished as the first and the last was quite in keeping with the similar distinction given just before between *"the first man Adam"* and *"the last Adam"* (1 Cor. 15:45), where, not a series, but two beings only are in view. The first trump was an announcement of condemnation, the last will be an announcement of emancipation. The first proclaimed a curse and threatened with death, the last will proclaim the blessing of immortal life. The first separated the terror-stricken hearers from the presence of God, the last will bring the saints to their Saviour in the joy of perfect union.

"So thus in Him accepted, and made meet
To share His glory bright,
We'll see His face and worship at His feet—
A day without a night."

"For I would not, brethren, that ye should be ignorant of **this mystery**, lest ye should be wise in your own conceits; **that blindness in part is happened to Israel, until the fulness of the Gentiles be come in**. And so all Israel shall be saved: as it is written, There shall come out of Sion the Deliverer, and shall turn away ungodliness from Jacob: For this is my covenant unto them, when I shall take away their sins. As concerning the gospel, they are enemies for your sakes: but as touching the election, they are beloved for the fathers' sakes. For the gifts and calling of God are without repentance. For as ye in times past have not believed God, yet have now obtained mercy through their unbelief: Even so have these also now not believed, that through your mercy they also may obtain mercy. For God hath concluded them all in unbelief, that he might have mercy upon all." Romans 11:25-32

CHAPTER EIGHT

The Hardening of Israel

Romans 11:25-32

The next group of mysteries for our consideration is of a different character from all that have preceded. We have grouped together the three which speak of departure from God and rejection of His revealed will. The first of the three relates to Israel; the second to corrupt religious systems; the third to the world.

The first, which forms the subject of this character, is mentioned in the Epistle to the Romans. Romans presents the gospel as the need it meets, the Person it proclaims, and the effects it produces. In the first eight chapters the subject is viewed in its application to every man, Jew or Gentile, without distinction. All are shown to be guilty before God; all, therefore, need salvation, which is offered to all on God's terms of grace through faith in Christ. In the next three chapters the apostle pursues the theme from the national and dispensational standpoints, reconciling the preceding foundation truths with God's promises to Israel.

ISRAEL NOT CAST OFF

After declaring the absolute sovereignty of God in His designs and dealings, and showing how His admission of Gentiles into the blessings of salvation through Christ was consistent alike with His counsels of election and with His pledges to Israel, Paul proceeds, in the eleventh chapter, to prove in three ways that God has not cast off His ancient people. Firstly, He has not cast them off totally. Paul himself is an Israelite, an example of the fact that, as in Elijah's day there was a remnant of faithful ones, so now "...*there is a remnant according to the election of grace*" (Rom. 11:5). Secondly, He has not cast them off for ever. Though the rest of the nation are hardened, and are suffering the retribution of a spirit of stupor, yet their condition is not irretrievable. On the contrary, "...*through their fall salvation is come unto the Gentiles*" (Rom. 11:11). And, so far from absolutely rejecting them, God has done this to provoke them to jealousy (vv. 7-11). Thirdly, their Deliverer shall yet come and turn away their ungodliness. And if their temporary rejection has meant reconciliation for Gentiles, how much greater will be the result of their reception! The nation is still the Lord's. The firstfruit is holy; then the last lump must be. The root of the olive tree is holy; then the branches are too. Some have been broken off, and others, wild branches, have, contrary to nature, been grafted into their own tree!

THE MYSTERY AND ITS MOTIVE

Now this interweaving of the counsels of God toward Jew and Gentile comprehends a mystery which Paul here makes known in confirmation of his preceding argument: "*For I would not, brethren, that ye should be ignorant of this mystery, lest ye should be wise in your own conceits; that blindness in part is happened to Israel, until the fulness of the Gentiles be come in. And so all Israel shall be saved*" (Rom. 11:25-26). The declaration of this mystery was calculated to prevent a spirit of self-complacency on the part of the Gentiles which might result in a similar retribution to that suffered by the Jews. The severity of God toward the latter and His consequent goodness towards the Gentiles should lead them not to high-mindedness but to fear.

THE MYSTERY AND ITS MEANING

The mystery consists, not in the fact that Israel will be restored to divine favour and blessing—Old Testament promises had assured that—but in the partial hardening of Israel until the fullness of the Gentiles has come in. Thus there are two limitations to this hardening, one of extent, the other of duration. As to extent, the nation has not been hardened in its entirety. The apostle has pointed out that there was a remnant according to the election of grace, and that the rest of the nation was hardened (Rom. 11:5-7). As to duration a definite time-limit is set, marked by the coming in of the fullness of the Gentiles. We must now consider the significance of this.

THE FULNESS OF THE GENTILES

The expression cannot mean the blessing of Gentile nations as a whole, for that will be consequent upon the salvation of Israel, whereas the fullness of the Gentiles is to be preliminary to it. Nor is it equivalent to "the times of the Gentiles", the period during which world-dominion is allotted to the Gentile powers, for neither the phraseology nor the context is suited to that meaning. Again, there is nothing in the passage to indicate that the consummation of Gentile iniquity is intended. The word *"fulness"* has just been used by the apostle to speak of blessing (Rom. 11:12). He has been showing, too, how God's mercy has brought salvation to Gentiles. When the number of the Gentiles who are to have part in the blessing of salvation in this dispensation is complete, the *"fulness"* will have "come in", and subsequently Israel will be saved. This seems to be the meaning intended according to the context.

A DISTINCTION

The fullness of the Gentiles is not quite the same thing as the church. For those Jews who have accepted Christ have thereby become part of the church, and these are distinguished from Gentiles in this passage, though in Christ there is neither Jew nor Gentile. Paul is not here speaking of the church, but of the dispensational dealings of God with Jew and Gentile, of His judicial severity towards the former, His goodness towards the latter, and the present common blessing held out to all. The apostle shows, too, that Israel's salvation is not only subsequent to, but consequent upon, God's present mercy to Gentiles: *"For as ye* (i.e., Gentiles) *in times past have not believed God, yet have now obtained mercy through their unbelief: Even so have these also now not believed, that through your mercy* (literally it is 'even so these now have been disobedient to your mercy, in order that') *they also may obtain mercy"* (Rom. 11:30-31). The immutable designs and all-controlling power of the will of God condition the motives and actions of humanity.

PAUL'S DOXOLOGY

Mercy is the paramount theme in the whole passage. There is no salvation by works either for Gentile or Jew, either for individual or nation. *"For God hath concluded them all in unbelief, that he might have mercy upon all"* (Rom. 11:32). Who that has experienced the saving mercies of our God, and looks forward to the day of Israel's deliverance and the glory of Israel's Messiah, can refrain from joining in the apostle's doxology:

> *"O the depth of the riches both of the wisdom and knowledge of God! how unsearchable are his judgments, and his ways past finding out! For who hath known the mind of the Lord? or who hath been his counsellor? Or who hath first given to him, and it shall be recompensed unto him again? For of him, and through him, and to him, are all things: to whom be glory for ever. Amen."*   Romans 11:33-36

"And there came one of the seven angels which had the seven vials, and talked with me, saying unto me, Come hither; I will shew unto thee the judgment of the great whore that sitteth upon many waters: With whom the kings of the earth have committed fornication, and the inhabitants of the earth have been made drunk with the wine of her fornication. So he carried me away in the spirit into the wilderness: and I saw a woman sit upon a scarlet coloured beast, full of names of blasphemy, having seven heads and ten horns. And the woman was arrayed in purple and scarlet colour, and decked with gold and precious stones and pearls, having a golden cup in her hand full of abominations and filthiness of her fornication: And upon her forehead was a name written, MYSTERY, BABYLON THE GREAT, THE MOTHER OF HARLOTS AND ABOMINATIONS OF THE EARTH." Revelation 17:1-5

CHAPTER NINE

The Mystery of Babylon
Revelation 17:1-5

This is the second of the group of mysteries relating to apostasy from God. In the vision recorded in Revelation 17 John was called to behold *"...the judgment of the great whore that sitteth upon many waters: With whom the kings of the earth have committed fornication, and the inhabitants of the earth have been made drunk with the wine of her fornication"* (Rev. 17:1-2). A woman was seen, gorgeously arrayed, holding a cup of abominations, and sitting *"...upon a scarlet coloured beast, full of names of blasphemy, having seven heads and ten horns"* (Rev. 17:3). Inscribed upon her forehead was the title, *"MYSTERY, BABYLON THE GREAT, THE MOTHER OF HARLOTS AND ABOMINATIONS OF THE EARTH"* (Rev. 17:5). *"And I saw,"* says the apostle, *"the woman drunken with the blood of the saints, and with the blood of the martyrs of Jesus"* (Rev. 17:6). In the interpretation of the symbols the woman is identified with Rome: *"And the woman which thou sawest is that great city, which reigneth over the kings of the earth"* (Rev. 17:18). Rome was thus immediately and prospectively the seat of Babylonish evil. The name of the woman was, however, associated with Babylon as a mystery, indicating that there were facts concerning Babylon which had not hitherto been revealed, and that the time had now come for the development and issues of the evils connected with it to be made known to the saints; indicating also that which would be developed in Rome was derived from the Chaldean city. We must therefore review the origin and history of that place.

BABYLON: ITS ORIGIN AND HISTORY

Babylon, the ancient Babel, was built under sinister conditions. The record of the motives with which men founded it makes clear that they did so regardless of God. Their designs were to establish a lasting monument of their energy and prowess—in the words of Scripture, *"let us make us a name"* (Gen. 11:4) —and, further, to provide a unifying centre by which to counteract the disintegrating tendencies which were manifesting themselves amidst humanity. To reckon without God is to court disaster. Divine retribution was speedy. Their language was confounded, their aims were thwarted, the building operations ceased, and the people were scattered (Gen. 11:1-9).

The city shortly afterwards became the scene of a second attempt at unity, now in a different way, yet still without recognition of God. Nimrod was apparently the first man to set up a kingdom in the earth. Having won fame among his fellows he seems to have conceived the idea of attempting to repair the disorder caused by the confusion of tongues by uniting men under himself. *"And the beginning of his kingdom was Babel, and Erech, and Accad, and Calneh, in the land of Shinar"* (Gen. 10:10). From thence he invaded Assyria, which belonged to the descendants of Shem, and built Nineveh and the other towns (v. 11; not as A.V.; see R.V.; an alternative rendering is "having become strong, he went forth and built Nineveh"). Babel, however, was his capital.[2]

SYSTEMATISED IDOLATRY

Modern discoveries which confirm the foregoing also show that Nimrod and his Queen, Semiramis, instituted a great system of idolatry. Nature worship was probably existent prior to this, but it was now systematised, and accompanied by elaborate rites and ceremonies performed by an order of priests.

Nimrod's power was thus both political and religious. By this combination he established a precedent which has had numerous followers. Again and again political ends have been served by usurping domination over the religious element in man. Control the conscience and you control the man. Temporal power is doubly strong if it combines

---

2   The events recorded in Genesis 11:1-9 chronologically precede those of chapter 10:10, 11. The tenth chapter is occupied with the genealogy of the descendants of Noah. The opening of the eleventh chapter is recapitulatory.

spiritual power with it. One of the most notable instances is that of the Emperor Constantine, who, in the fourth century of the present era, gained by this means his ascendency in the Roman world.

At his death Nimrod was deified as the sun-god, and Semiramis thereupon inaugurated the worship of a trinity—father, mother, and son. After her death she was venerated as "Queen of Heaven", and the sun-god came to be regarded as her child. Thus mother and son became the prominent deities.[3]

ORGANIZED REBELLION

That such organized rebellion against God should emanate from Babel is high significant. We know from Genesis 4 that this was the region where Satan made his first attack upon the soul of man. Here man was first taught to substitute his own will for God's. It may be that this very spot was the scene of the temptation of Adam and Eve. It now became the centre from which the evils of idolatry were to disseminate throughout the earth. Satan, anticipating the incarnation of the Son of God, and the time when the Seed of the woman would bruise his head, initiated the worship of mother and child with a view to nullifying the redemptive work of God through Christ.

The system, inaugurated at Babel, remained in the different nations that were scattered from thence, though in the course of time tradition led to considerable variation of detail. The common origin, however, explains such facts as this, that when the emissaries of popery entered heathen lands for the inculcation of that religion they found that many of the papal rites and ceremonies had been existent there already from time immemorial. Prescott, in his work on Peru, says, "One is astonished to find so close a resemblance between the institution of the American Indian, the ancient Roman, and the modern Catholic". The fact is that all three and many other institutions are easily traceable to the same Babylonian source, the pristine idolatries of Babel.

---

3   Compare Job 31:26-28, and Jeremiah 44:17, 25

FROM BABYLON TO ROME

We must now trace further the course of the Babylonian system, noticing the manner in which the church became corrupted by it, and the judgment which God has appointed for it.

For many centuries after the nation had been scattered from Babel that city remained the seat of the cult which had been systematised in the time of Nimrod. When in 539 B.C. Cyrus, the Persian monarch, captured Babylon, the Chaldean priests were expelled, and fled to Asia Minor. Here they found a refuge under the king of the Lydian realm, by whom they were welcomed, and at whose capital, Pergamos, their hierarchy was established. At this city they and their successors continued during the period of the Grecian rule, which succeeded that of the Persians. Satan's throne was thus moved from Babylon to Pergamos. This is doubtless the point of the reference to Pergamos as Satan's throne in the letter to the church in that town, as recorded in Revelation 2:13. At the death of Attalus III, the last of the Lydian kings, in 133 B.C., his kingdom, and the Chaldean priesthood with it, passed under the dominion of the Romans. From Pergamos Julius Caesar, in the next century, removed the priests and all their paraphernalia to Rome. This he did for political reasons. Already as head of the Roman State he had accepted from the people the priestly office of Pontifex Maximus, i.e., the chief Pontiff[4] of the pagan religion of Rome; and now, combining in himself the double power of political and religious authority over the Republic, his ends would be well served by incorporating under his high-priesthood the Chaldean system with which he had become acquainted in the Lydian kingdom. The gorgeous ritual of the Chaldean priests would add splendour and influence to the Roman religion. Thus did Rome become the seat of the Babylonian abominations. That is clearly indicated at the close of the interpretation given in Revelation 17, concerning the woman upon whose brow the name of Babylon was inscribed: *"the woman which thou sawest*

---

4   The heathen origin of this title, as retained by the Popes, is thus obvious.

is that great city, which reigneth over the kings of the earth" (Rev. 17:18). Rome was thus pointed out to the apostle as the chief centre of the religious system which had its rise in Babylon.

SATANIC STRATEGY AGAINST CHRISTIANITY

To move the centre of opposition to God and to His truth westward was a piece of Satanic strategy. Satan seems to have known that the testimony of the gospel would make progress chiefly westward; he accordingly shifted his point of vantage in a corresponding direction. The Roman world was permeated beforehand with the teachings of the Chaldean system, as a preparation for the corruption of the church, when it should decline from its loyalty to its Head. This apostasy of the church, having developed after the times of the apostles, continued with increasing rapidity through the second and third centuries of this era, until everything was ready for the complete amalgamation of paganism with Christianity. It simply required a man of sufficient genius and power to weld the two together.

CONSTANTINE THE GREAT

Early in the fourth century the man appeared in the person of the Emperor Constantine, to whom reference has already been made. Aspirations after supremacy in the Roman Empire, and the desire to unite its disintegrating elements, led him to adopt what was obviously the wisest policy to attain this end. The church had become politically influential. Forsaking the path marked out for it by its Founder it had attained worldly greatness, and was an organization to be reckoned with by any aspirant after world-power. What could suit Constantine's aim better than to make Christianity (such as it had become) a State religion? Chaldean doctrines and rites had already been preached and practised in many churches, and the Chaldean cult was the general religion of the pagans. Amalgamation was easy. It practically materialized at the council of bishops summoned by the Emperor at Nicaea in Asia Minor in A.D. 325. Thereafter popery blossomed out in all its fullness. The history of the adaptation of the Babylonish rites and festivals to Christianity is fully given in Hislop's "Two Babylons".[5] The circumstances by which the harlot church, disloyal to Christ, and in unholy union with the world's religion and the world's political affairs, found its headquarters in Rome, are well known to readers of history.

THE MOTHER AND HER HARLOT DAUGHTERS

We must distinguish between the woman and that which is signified by the name written on her forehead. The woman is clearly identified with Rome, as we have seen; her name shows her Babylonish origin. Mystic Babylon is not the woman. Babylon as a mystery is "...*MYSTERY, BABYLON THE GREAT, THE MOTHER OF HARLOTS AND ABOMINATIONS OF THE EARTH*" (Rev. 17:5). Of these harlot-daughters Romanism is one. But Babylon is the mother of every form of abomination. All religion in which the worship of the creature is substituted for the worship of the Creator springs from Babylon. Nature-worship, both in its baser and its less repulsive forms, had its home there. Many of the philosophic theories, both of ancient and modern times, are traceable to the same source, and particularly, the view that man sprang from the Godhead, and that by working out his destiny by self-effort he will eventually be perfected in the Godhead. This is one of the main teachings of Spiritism and of Buddhism, with its modernized form, Theosophy, as well as many other false religions. Theosophy, Spiritism necromancy, fetishism, demon-worship, Devil-worship, and every similar species of evil had their origin in that prime centre of rebellion against God. Thither can be traced the worship of the Virgin. From Babylon have come priestcraft, and every form of ecclesiasticism and clerisy in which man takes the place of Christ. If the origin and history of Babylon are rightly understood, and the connection between Babylon, and the spiritual mystery of Revelation 17, and Babylon the centre of commerce of Revelation 18, is apprehended, then the truth

---

5   S.W. Partidge & Co., London

of the statement with which the eighteenth chapter ends can be readily grasped, namely, that *"in her was found the blood of prophets, and of saints, and of all that were slain upon the earth"* (Rev. 18:24). For religion and commerce have been responsible for cruelty and oppression, persecution and bloodshed, from Nimrod's day till now.

THE WOMAN ON THE BEAST

While the name on the woman indicates her origin and character, the woman herself is symbolic in two respects, topographically with the city of Rome, and mystically with the amalgamated forms of ecclesiasticism which have their centre there. For the woman rides the seven headed and ten-horned beast; and the beast is, firstly, the political and civil power of the Roman Empire,[6] which in its final form will exist as a league of ten nations (Rev. 17:12).[7] Inasmuch as the woman rides the beast, the amalgamation of the religious systems of what is known as Christendom will apparently result in the revived influence and power of Romanism for a brief period. The destruction of the whole ecclesiastical system has been clearly foretold. It will receive its overthrow at the hands of the political world over which its influence has been exercised. *"And the ten horns which thou sawest upon the beast, these shall hate the whore, and shall make her desolate and naked, and shall eat her flesh, and burn her with fire"* (Rev. 17:16).

THE MYSTERY MADE KNOWN

The mystery of Babylon had been kept hid through the long centuries of its history, from the time of Babel till the close of the days of the apostles, when the church was just about to come under its Satanic influence. Then was the truth made known to the saints through the revelation given to John, first to the seven churches in Asia, to which the whole

---

6   See *"The Roman Empire in Prophecy"*, by W. E. Vine. Pickering & Inglis, London, Glasgow, and Edinburgh

7   The symbolic term "beast" stands, in the 17th chapter of Revelation, secondly, for the ultimate federal head of the league. For this association of the dominion and its chief potentate, under the one symbol, compare Daniel 7:17 and 23.

book of the Revelation was sent, and since then to all to whom it is granted "to read and to hear the words of this prophecy, and to keep the things which are written therein".

(e)
Mysteries Relating to the Consummation of the Purposes of God

"Now we beseech you, brethren, by the coming of our Lord Jesus Christ, and by our gathering together unto him, That ye be not soon shaken in mind, or be troubled, neither by spirit, nor by word, nor by letter as from us, as that the day of Christ is at hand. Let no man deceive you by any means: for that day shall not come, except there come a falling away first, and that man of sin be revealed, the son of perdition; Who opposeth and exalteth himself above all that is called God, or that is worshipped; so that he as God sitteth in the temple of God, shewing himself that he is God. Remember ye not, that, when I was yet with you, I told you these things? And now ye know what withholdeth that he might be revealed in his time." 2 Thessalonians 2:1-6

CHAPTER TEN

The Mystery of Lawlessness

2 Thessalonians 2:1-6

This mystery, the third and last of the group relating to the rebellion against God, is dealt win in the Second Epistle to the Thessalonians, in a passage in which Paul is correcting their mistaken views as to the Coming, or Parousia, of the Lord Jesus and the Day of the Lord. Between these two events, or rather epochs, he draws a distinction, which forbids their being identified. In the interests of the right opinions of his readers about the former (chap. 2:1, R.V., margin, "on behalf of")[8] he now shows that the latter, a period of God's judgments in the earth, had not already set in, as they had been led to believe. Certain events in the world must precede that, events connected with the Mystery of Lawlessness.

THE ORIGIN OF LAWLESSNESS

Before speaking of those events we must consider the meaning of the phrase, "The Mystery of Lawlessness". It does not indicate that the lawlessness referred to is something mysterious or working in a mysterious way. There is no mystery, in the ordinary sense of the term, attaching to lawlessness itself, which simply consists of the repudiation of law, whether divine or human. The "Mystery of Lawlessness" is, however, something more than this. As one of the mysteries of Scripture, as something, that is, which lies beyond human understanding, and thus can become known only by divine revelation, lawlessness is the outcome of a settled plan on the part of Satan and his hosts to overthrow God's government. The spirit of independence of God, and of refusal to accept His revealed will and way, is directed by the prince of the

---

8   The Greek preposition *luper* should be rendered "in the interests of"; the Revised Version margin, "on behalf of", is equivalent.

power of the air who *"worketh in the children of disobedience"* (Eph. 2:2). His aim is to shut out God, dethrone Christ, and exalt man in His place under his own control.

How little do men realize that at the back of the world's movements is the arch-opponent of God, who is goading it on to its climax of rebellion against the Most High and to its consequent judgment! Yet so it is. To the one, however, who, having bowed to the authority of Christ, intelligently reads the Scriptures, the truths of this mystery become increasingly clear, and especially as he sees them confirmed by the trend of events in the world. Men of the world may judge of lawlessness by the actual effects as seen at the time; the spiritual source and development and issues are revealed only to the saints.

THE MEANING OF LAWLESSNESS

Further, lawlessness is not necessarily confusion and disorder. Even religion and morality may be characterized by a repudiation of God's counsels and claims as made known in His Word, and, accordingly, may themselves constitute lawlessness. This was taught by the Lord in the Sermon on the Mount. He showed that it is possible to call Him "Lord" and yet not to do the will of His Father. *"Many,"* He says, *"will say to me in that day, Lord, Lord, have we not prophesied in thy name? and in thy name have cast out devils? and in thy name done many wonderful works? And then will I profess unto them, I never knew you: depart from me, ye that work iniquity"* (Matt. 7:22-23; the word is the same in the original as in 2 Thess. 2:7). Lawlessness, then, is disregard of the will of God. Self-will may either act along the moral and religious plane, or break out in open-handed rebellion against God. In each case men are guilty of lawlessness.

THE MAN OF LAWLESSNESS

Let us see now what the apostle has to say about the Mystery of Lawlessness. He tells the Thessalonian saints that the Day of the Lord (i.e., the period ushered in by the Second Advent of Christ in His manifested glory) will not commence until the falling away has come (*i.e.,* a general departure from God and His Word), and the *"man of sin* (Man of Lawlessness, R.V. margin) *be revealed, the son of perdition; Who opposeth and exalteth himself above all that is called God, or that is worshipped; so that he as God sitteth in the temple of God, shewing himself that he is God"* (2 Thess. 2:3-4). He is called in verse 8 *"the lawless one"* (NKJV), i.e., he will be the greatest human expression, the very embodiment, of lawlessness. The world, moreover, will be ripe for the advent and reception of this emissary of Satan.

Meanwhile the mystery of lawlessness was already working in the apostle's time, and has been working ever since, only it has been under restraint, and Paul states that this has been imposed in order that the Man of Sin may be revealed at the proper season. May not this suggest that Satan would have produced him earlier but for the restraint exercised? Paul does not specify to the Thessalonians what this is—doubtless to avoid giving their enemies a ground of making a political charge against them. He describes the restraining power in two ways, first as a principle, "that which restraineth", second as a person, "one that restraineth" (2 Thess. 2:6-7). The person evidently embodies the principle. The restraint would continue until the power exercising it would be taken (lit., "become") out of the way, the result being the revelation of the lawless one.

THE RESTRAINER

It is only needful to mention two of the suggested explanations as to this restraining power.[9] One is that the restrainer is the Holy Spirit, acting through the church; at the rapture of the church the Holy Spirit will be taken away from the earth. There are several objections to that explanation. The other is that the restraining principle is that of the constituted government, which is always embodied in the highest ruler in the State, and was represented in Paul's time by the Emperor

---

9   See "The Epistles to the Thessalonians, with Notes Exegetical and Expository", by Messrs. Hogg and Vine. Pickering & Inglis (4/6).

at Rome. The phrase "one that restraineth" is, literally, "the restrainer", and so may stand for a number of individuals presenting the same characteristics, just as "the believer" stands for all believers.

"THE POWERS THAT BE"

That such constituted authority is at all times a great restraining power against lawlessness is clear (a) from facts of Scripture history (see Acts 17:9; 18:12-17; 19:40; 21:27-36; 25:6-12); (b) from the doctrine of Scripture (see Rom. 13:1-7; 1 Tim. 2:2; 1 Pet. 2:13-17); and (c) from facts of the history of nations up to the present day. When constituted government in any country has been overthrown by revolutionary mobs, lawlessness has been broken loose from the great restraint which controlled it. So it was in the French Revolution. So it is today in Russia and Germany. What is Bolshevism but lawlessness that disregards the authority of God, would overthrow all forms of government that He has ordained for the maintenance of peace and order, and retain its power by anarchy? Are not the evidences abundant that in Christendom itself restraint is being thrown off and lawlessness is spreading with great rapidity? If constitutional government is overthrown in a still more general way, the laws of God for man are repudiated still more widely, the situation will be fully ripe for the advent of the lawless one.

THE CLIMAX OF LAWLESSNESS

In whatever way lawlessness spreads, whether by anarchy or by bloodless revolutions, Satan is rapidly preparing the ground for the production of his human masterpiece. Whatever the restraining power may be—and it certainly appears to be considerably weakened at the present time—it will be removed, and the Man of Sin will arise to take control of men and of affairs.

His period of power will be brief. The Satanic scheme for the world-wide dominion of man, under his rule, and in rebellion against God and His Christ, will be upset. A stronger than the strong man armed will come and bind him and spoil his goods. *"And then the lawless one will be revealed, whom the Lord will consume with the breath of His mouth and destroy with the brightness of His coming"* (2 Thess. 2:8, NKJV). Lawlessness will then yield place to righteousness under the benign yet firm government of God's King, the Son to whom the Father says: *"Thou hast loved righteousness, and hated iniquity"* (Heb. 1:9). God hasten the Day of His glory in the earth, when He shall reign in righteousness and equity from sea to sea!

*"And I saw another mighty angel come down from heaven, clothed with a cloud: and a rainbow was upon his head, and his face was as it were the sun, and his feet as pillars of fire: And he had in his hand a little book open: and he set his right foot upon the sea, and his left foot on the earth, And cried with a loud voice, as when a lion roareth: and when he had cried, seven thunders uttered their voices. And when the seven thunders had uttered their voices, I was about to write: and I heard a voice from heaven saying unto me, Seal up those things which the seven thunders uttered, and write them not. And the angel which I saw stand upon the sea and upon the earth lifted up his hand to heaven, And sware by him that liveth for ever and ever...But in the days of the voice of the seventh angel, when he shall begin to sound, the **mystery of God** should be finished, as he hath declared to his servants the prophets."*

Revelation 10:1-7

CHAPTER ELEVEN

The Mystery of God's Purposes in Judgment

Revelation 10:1-7

The subject of this Mystery is connected with the series of revelations given to the apostle John concerning the judgments of God in the earth at the close of the present age. The seventh seal had been opened, the sixth trumpet had sounded, and, after the events immediately following the latter, the apostle saw a strong angel coming down out of heaven, arrayed with a cloud, a rainbow upon his head, his face as the sun, his feet as pillars of fire, and a little book open in his hand. Setting his right foot upon the sea and his left upon the earth, the angel cried with a great voice as of a lion. Upon this seven thunders pealed forth, but the significance of their messages was withheld. He then lifted up his right hand to heaven, and *"sware by him that liveth for ever and ever, who created heaven, and the things that therein are, and the earth, and the things that therein are, and the sea, and the things which are therein, that there should be time no longer: But in the days of the voice of the seventh angel, when he shall begin to sound, the mystery of God should be finished, as he hath declared to his servants the prophets"* (Rev. 10:6-7).

THE PLACE OF THE MYSTERY

It is necessary to observe the place which the blowing of the seventh trumpet has in the series of revelations relating to the seals, the trumpets, and the vials. The opening of the seals embraces the whole series of judgments from beginning to end. The blowing of the trumpets embraces all that are included under the seventh seal, and describes in greater detail the judgements under that seal. Again, the blowing of the seventh trumpet introduces the closing series of judgments inflicted by the seven last plagues poured forth from the seven vials or bowls (Rev. 15 and 16). *"...the seven last plagues, for in them the wrath of God is complete"* (Rev. 15:1, NKJV).

The close of chapter 11, giving details of the blowing of the seventh trumpet, is connected with the close of chapter 16. In chapter 11 the blowing of the seventh trumpet is followed first by voices announcing that *"...The kingdoms of this world are become the kingdoms of our Lord, and of his Christ"* (Rev. 11:15), and then by the worship of the four and twenty elders, who declare that the final judgments have come, and the exercise of God's regal power in the earth. The events that are mentioned in verse 19 commence the carrying out of those declarations. The temple of God is opened in heaven, and there follow in the earth *"...lightnings, and voices, and thunderings, and an earthquake, and great hail"* (Rev. 11:19).

Compare now the end of chapter 16, describing the pouring out of the seventh bowl. A great voice comes out of the temple from the throne, saying *"It is done"*(Rev. 16:17). Then follow lightnings, and voices, and thunders—a great and unprecedented earthquake and great hail. The two passages evidently point to the same occasion. The intervening chapters 12 to 14 deal with relative events from other standpoints.

A DISTINCTION

These considerations help us to understand the declarations in chapter 10 by the angel who was seen standing on the sea and the earth, and who sware that there shall be delay no longer, but that *"in the days of the voice of the seventh angel, when he shall begin[10] to sound, (the last of the seven trumpets), the mystery of God should be finished"* (Rev. 10:7).

This Mystery, accordingly, has to do with the execution of God's judgments in the earth. It is thus to be distinguished

---

10 The word in the original is not adequately rendered by either *"is about"* (R.V.) or *"begin"*. It frequently signifies, and obviously here, the "fixed necessity or Divine appointment" by which and event is come to pass. See Grimm-Thayer's Lexicon, μέλλω, 2.0.

from *"the mystery of God"* mentioned in Colossians 2:2, which has formed the subject of our previous consideration. That Mystery relates to the Godhead of Christ. In other words, *"the mystery of God"* in Colossians 2:2 is subjective, and concerns the Person Himself, that in Revelation 10:7 is objective, and concerns His dealings with men.

WHY A MYSTERY?

In what respect does this latter constitute a Mystery? The answer seems to be first in the fact that since *"...the whole world lies under the sway of the wicked one"* (1 John 5:19), who is its god, its disregard of the claims of God pursues a course of lawlessness, until a culmination is reached in the banding together of humanity under its then satanically-controlled rulers (for these, see Rev. 13) in open-handed rebellion against the Most High. Consequently the saints are now the object of the Devil's malignity, and righteousness suffers. But God is not indifferent to it all. Since mercy and slowness to anger are essentials of His character, His longsuffering waits, and He stays the execution of His wrath. At the same time He holds lawlessness under a measure of restraint. At length , however, *"the day of the LORD's vengeance"* (Isa. 34:8) and *"the year of my redeemed"* (Isa. 63:4) will arrive. The vials of His wrath will be poured out in rapid succession. Those that destroy the earth will themselves be destroyed by His power. The government of the world will be wrested from the cruel hand of Satan by the Conqueror who defeated him at Calvary, and *"the kingdoms of this world are become the kingdoms of our Lord, and of his Christ"* (Rev. 11:15).

THE COMPLETION OF THE MYSTERY

This, then, is *"...the mystery of God...as He declared to His servants the prophets"* (Rev. 10:7, NKJV)—a mystery hidden in past ages, but made known to those who have already bowed in allegiance to the Son of God. The mystery is said to be finished at the time referred to, because all the prophecies concerning this age and the intervention of God at its close will then have had fulfilment. As in the pouring forth of the vials the wrath of God is finished (Rev. 16:1), so in the overthrow of unrighteousness, and the establishment of the Kingdom of righteousness, the mystery of God will be finished. The good tidings are those which proclaim the triumph of Christ in the deliverance of the groaning creation and the inauguration of His reign of peace.

A POINT OF CONNECTION

There is a deeply interesting point of connection between the mystery of God mentioned in the Colossian Epistle and that mentioned in Revelation 10:7: *"But in the days of the voice of the seventh angel, when he shall begin to sound, the mystery of God should be finished, as he hath declared to his servants the prophets."* This lies in the fact that both are apparently to be completed at the same time.

The mystery of God which forms the subject of the second chapter of Colossians has to do first with the Godhead of Christ in His relationship to the Father, and then with the union with Him of all believers as the church which is His body. The apostle combines these two relationships thus, *"For in him dwelleth all the fulness of the Godhead bodily. And ye are complete in him"* (Col. 2:9-10).[11]

Now when the church is complete and has been caught up to meet the Lord at the commencement of His Parousia, it is destined, after certain events have taken place in the heavenlies, to come forth with Him in the revelation of His glory to the world. This will be the shining forth of the Parousia, i.e., of His presence with His saints.[12] *"He shall come to be glorified in his saints, and to be admired in all them that believe"* (2 Thess. 1:10). The world, which has refused to acknowledge Him; will then be compelled to recognize His Godhead, and will witness the glorious union of the church with its Redeemer. That mystery of God will be thus in full evidence.

---

11 The Revised Version rightly replaces the full stop between the two verses by a comma. Verses 9 and 10 are continuations of verses 2 and 3, the intervening portion being a parenthetic warning and exhortation.

12 See *"Touching the Coming of the Lord"*, by C. F. Hogg and W. E. Vine.

THE SIMULTANEOUS TERMINATION OF
THE MYSTERIES OF GOD

Simultaneously with this the other *"mystery of God"*, relating to His judgments in the earth, will be completed. As we have already seen, this latter mystery is to be finished when the judgments which follow the blowing of the seventh trumpet, and which consist of the pouring out of the wrath of God from the seven vials, are executed.

Thus the revelation of the first mystery of God, and the completion of the second, will take place together. For the final judgment, at the end of this age, is to be executed at the pouring forth of the seventh vial, by the direct intervention of the Son of Man when He comes in the clouds of heaven to overthrow His foes in the climax of their Satanic efforts against God and against His people the Jews. At that personal intervention all His saints will be present with Him.

"Blessed be the God and Father of our Lord Jesus Christ, who hath blessed us with all spiritual blessings in heavenly places in Christ: According as he hath chosen us in him before the foundation of the world, that we should be holy and without blame before him in love: Having predestinated us unto the adoption of children by Jesus Christ to himself, according to the good pleasure of his will, To the praise of the glory of his grace, wherein he hath made us accepted in the beloved. In whom we have redemption through his blood, the forgiveness of sins, according to the riches of his grace; Wherein he hath abounded toward us in all wisdom and prudence; Having made known unto us the mystery of his will, according to his good pleasure which he hath purposed in himself: That in the dispensation of the fulness of times he might gather together in one all things in Christ, both which are in heaven, and which are on earth; even in him."

Ephesians 1:3-10

CHAPTER TWELVE

The Mystery of God's Will

Ephesians 1:3-10

After the ascription of praise with which the apostle Paul commences his Epistle to the Ephesians, he relates the blessings with which God has blessed us in the heavenly places, according to the riches of His grace, and then declares the mystery of His will from the dispensational standpoint. This God has made known to us *"in all wisdom and prudence"* (Eph. 1:8).[13]

The development of revelation in the Scriptures is one of their profoundest features. The purposes of God concerning the dispensations are therein made known by a gradual progression of expanding revelations. Similarly by a gradual unfolding the Lord imparted truths to His disciples. On the eve of His crucifixion He said to them, *"I have yet many things to say unto you, but ye cannot bear them now"* (John 16:12). The Spirit of Truth would guide them into all the truth. In His wisdom and prudence He arranged the time and manner of the communication of the divine counsels. Thus it is with the mystery of God's will.

THE UNIVERSE RECONSTITUTED

The mystery is said to be *"...according to his good pleasure which he hath purposed in himself:*[14] *That in the dispensation* (literally 'an economy') *of the fulness of times*[15] *he might gather together in one all things in Christ, both which are in heaven, and which are on earth; even in him"* (Eph. 1:9-10).

---

13 Just as in verse 4 the words "in love" are perhaps to be connected with verse 5, so in verse 8 "in all wisdom and prudence" are apparently intended to go with "having made known unto us the mystery of His will".

14 That is to say, "in Christ", and not as rendered in Authorized Version.

15 Correctly translated this should be "the fullness of the seasons". "Times" are periods, "seasons" are epochs. The former denote lengths of time, and the latter signify that these periods have special characteristics or circumstances associated with them respectively.

What a vast vision is here disclosed to view! The universe is to be reconstituted in Christ. All things in the heavens and on the earth are to be reunited under His Headship. All the dispensations, or seasons, which have preceded have been preparatory to this great consummation. All the dealings of God which have characterized the various ages will receive their culmination in that age; hence it will be "the fullness of the seasons".

Christ will be the uniting bond of all things. In Him, through Him, and for Him were all things created (Col. 1:16). *"For it pleased the Father that in him should all fulness dwell; And, having made peace through the blood of his cross, by him to reconcile all things unto himself; by him, I say, whether they be things in earth, or things in heaven"* (Col. 1:19-20).

THE TIME OF RECONSTITUTION

In its universal character the first stage of this great reunion will take place at the inauguration of the millennial reign of Christ, that is to say, at the time when, as we have seen above, the mystery of God will have been finished. The destruction of Antichrist and his associates, the deliverance of the Jews from their oppressors, and the binding and removal of Satan will be followed by Messiah's reign of righteousness and peace. But this itself will be only a prelude to the complete fulfilment of the mystery of God's will in Christ. The consummation of all will take place in the age to follow, when, in the new heavens and earth, there will be no discordant element, nothing that is not absolutely adjusted to the will of God.

THE SPHERE OF RECONSTITUTION

We must not fail to observe that, while this gathers together in one all things in Christ extends to things in the heavens and things on the earth, it is not said to embrace *"things under the earth"*, the third sphere mentioned in Philippians 2:10. Paul's readers could not possibly have understood his words to mean the inclusion of this last realm. No ground is here afforded for the assumption—so frequently contradicted elsewhere in Scripture—that those who die in their sins will at length come within the scope of salvation. No warrant is given in this passage for any man to presume on the mercy of God, and to expect reconciliation in spite of unrepentance in this life. God's pardoning grace and a share in the glories that are to be revealed are offered freely to all men now, through the acceptance of His terms of grace in the redemption accomplished for us by the death of His Son for our sins. Should the reader not yet have received this great salvation he may today become the happy possessor of it through faith in Christ.

> *"Come, crown and throne; come, robe and palm;*
> *Burst forth glad stream of peace!*
> *Come holy city of the Lamb!*
> *Rise, Sun of Righteousness!"*

Index of Scripture

THE 12 MYSTERIES OF SCRIPTURE

INDEX OF SCRIPTURE

Other Books

by W. E. VINE, M.A.

The Roman Empire in the Light of Prophecy; or, The Rise, Progress, and End of the Fourth World-Empire. With maps and illustrations.

The Twelve Mysteries of the Bible: Studies in the Secrets of God, revealed in the Word.

Outlines of the Epistle of James: The Occasion, Objects, and Analysis of the Epistle. With 16 outline studies therein.

The Scriptures and How to Use Them: Suggestions for getting the most out of the Mine

B.C. and A.D.; or, How the World was prepared for the Gospel

ALSO IN COLLABORATION WITH C. F. HOGG

The Epistles to the Thessalonians: With Notes, Exegetical and Expository. With Index to Subject, Texts, and Greek Words. Commended by Lord Blythswood, Sir Robert Anderson, James F. Arthur, Theological Tutor, B.T.I. Glasgow; Geo. F. Trench, B.A.; H. M. Bleby, B.A.,&c.

Touching the Coming of the Lord: The Resurrection—The Rapture—The Parousia—The Judgment-Seat—The Epiphany, etc., with diagram.

"The Good Deposit" (2 Tim. 1:14; R.V.); A Restatement of some of the more important Christian Doctrines.

The Bitter Spirit: The Deadly Effects of Bitterness

by Paul Young

Bitterness is a deeply destructive emotion. It can develop in our spirits like infection in a wound. It can make us ineffective and useless for God's service and could undermine the work of our church. A bitter reaction will always undermine the integrity of the Gospel because the Gospel is a message that conquers bitterness.

The Lord Jesus took all our bitterness on the cross where He paid the ultimate price for sin. So in Christ we can find release from the bondage that bitterness produces. May God grant us the grace to always leave bitterness at the feet of the Saviour so that we can live life unburdened by the weight of a bitter spirit which ultimately will cause the most damage to ourselves.

To Be Like Jesus: Studies in the Fruit of the Spirit

by Paul Young

"But the fruit of the Spirit is love, joy, peace, patience, kindness, goodness, faithfulness, gentleness and self-control" (Gal. 5:22-23).

The New Testament places an abundance of emphasis upon Christian fruitfulness. Indeed Jesus says that we can recognize true Christians from those who are false by their fruit. He said, *"by their fruit you will recognize them"* (Matt. 7:20, NIV). So this is an important subject with strong implications for us.

We can also say that the fruit of the Spirit was most fully and most wonderfully witnessed in the life of the Lord Jesus. He is our example of someone who truly lived the fruit of the Spirit. We are called to walk in His footsteps, to be like Him and to show the nine-fold fruit of the Spirit in our lives.

Unless You Repent by H. A. Ironside

"It is especially timely that this book should be reprinted at this time. It deals with issues that are the subject of some misinformation and misunderstanding. Ironside's clear and gracious handling of the much misunderstood doctrine of repentance comes as a breath of fresh air, dispelling the fog."   William MacDonald

True Discipleship (with Study Guide)
by William MacDonald

Am I ignitable?

A disciple can be forgiven if he does not have great mental ability or physical prowess. But he cannot be excused if he does not have zeal. If his heart is not aflame with a red-hot passion for the Saviour, he stands condemned. After all, Christians are followers of the One who said, "Zeal for Your house has eaten Me up" (John. 2:17). Their Saviour was consumed with a passion for God and for his interests. Those who are constrained by the love of Christ will count no sacrifice too great to make for Him.

"This book is an attempt to highlight some principles of New Testament discipleship. Some of us have seen these principles in the Word for years, but somehow concluded that they were too extreme and impractical for the complicated age in which we live. And so we surrendered to the chill of our spiritual environment. Then we met a group of young believers who set out to demonstrate that the Savior's terms of discipleship are not only highly practical but that they are the only terms which will ever result in the evangelization of the world.

"To the extent that these truths are still beyond our own personal experience, we present them as the aspiration of our heart."   William MacDonald

CPSIA information can be obtained
at www.ICGtesting.com
Printed in the USA
FSOW02n1750150117
29496FS